CW01390316

To-

From—

Other mini giftbooks in this series:
Notebook for a very special Daughter
Notebook for a very special Friend
Notebook for a very special Grandmother
Notebook for a very special Husband
Notebook for a very special Sister

Published simultaneously in 1996 by Exley Giftbooks in
the USA and Exley Publications Ltd in Great Britain.

12 11 10 9 8 7 6 5 4 3 2 1

Copyright © Helen Exley 1996.
ISBN 1-85015-786-3

Edited by Helen Exley.
Written by Pam Brown.
Illustrated by Juliette Clarke.
Typeset by Delta, Watford.
Printed in Singapore.

Dedicated to Momtom: the most special mother of them all.

Exley Publications Ltd, 16 Chalk Hill, Watford, Herts WD1 4BN, UK
Exley Giftbooks, 232 Madison Avenue, Suite 1206, NY 10016, USA

NOTEBOOK

For a very special
MOTHER

Written by Pam Brown

Illustrated by Juliette Clarke

EXLEY

NEW YORK • WATFORD, UK

_____

_____

_____

_____

_____

_____

_____

_____

_____

_____

_____

_____

_____

_____

_____

_____

_____

Mothers are always on stand-by.

Only a mother can send hugs by post.

Mothers can do running repairs actually on the run.

_____

_____

_____

_____

_____

_____

_____

_____

_____

_____

_____

_____

_____

Only a mother can make Family out of an assortment of
disparate individuals.

Mothers are the only people who tell you the truth when it's going to hurt.

Only mothers have lists. That breed. And grow.

Mothers are the people who yell after you waving the things you've forgotten.

Mothers know when you are faking.

Thank you for "Try hard. Work hard. And if you can't do it, turn your attention to something else."
Saved a lot of heartache.

_____

_____

_____

_____

_____

_____

_____

_____

_____

_____

_____

_____

Thanks for never saying. "I told you so."
Well - not often.

_____

_____

_____

_____

_____

_____

_____

_____

_____

_____

_____

_____

_____

_____

_____

_____

_____

_____

_____

_____

Thank you for always being there.
Not intrusively. Not demandingly.
There.

_____

_____

_____

_____

_____

_____

_____

_____

_____

_____

_____

_____

_____

A mother is the person who hears when you are
grizzling silently into your pillow.

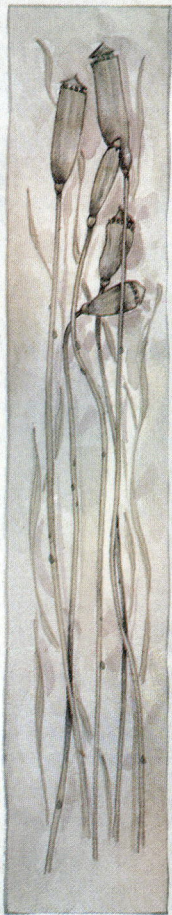

When it's sorrow beyond keeping,
phone home.

Love is exciting
But sometimes one needs a quiet
kitchen, a cup of coffee and one's mother.

Mothers can dry your tears down a telephone.

_____

_____

_____

_____

_____

_____

_____

_____

_____

_____

_____

_____

_____

_____

A mother has the magic glue that sticks the broken
pieces together.

I don't know how you fitted me in.
But you did.
And do.

Your life is so full - and yet I know that,
always, always,
There is room for me.

_____

_____

_____

_____

_____

_____

_____

_____

_____

_____

_____

_____

_____

_____

Mother love is the fuel that enables a normal human being
to do the impossible.

_____

_____

_____

_____

_____

_____

_____

_____

_____

_____

_____

_____

_____

_____

_____

_____

Mother love doesn't need as much sleep
as other sorts.

_____

_____

_____

_____

_____

_____

_____

_____

_____

_____

_____

_____

_____

Mother love doesn't give a damn about your looks.
She thinks you are beautiful, anyway.

Mother love is the family's pilot light.

Mothers don't really have premonitions. They have been
over every possible eventuality so often - both good and ill -
that whatever happens to you.
they've rehearsed it.

Mothers are inclined to worry. All the time.
Thanks, for not letting it show too much.

_____

_____

_____

_____

_____

_____

_____

_____

_____

_____

_____

_____

_____

_____

_____

_____

_____

_____

_____

_____

_____

_____

I love it when you are excited and pleased
because I've had a success or a stroke of luck.
And I love it all the more when you still think
I'm wonderful when I've fallen flat on my face.

Thanks for not giving up on me when I'd
been particularly awful. You were the only one
who didn't.

Thanks for opening all those doors for me -
but never shoving me through them.

Good mothers give their children paints and brushes and canvas, but let them paint their own picture.